THE BLUE WHALE

THE BLUE WHALE

THOMAS Y. CROWELL COMPANY
NEW YORK

BY KAZUE MIZUMURA

LET'S-READ-AND-FIND-OUT SCIENCE BOOKS

Editors: *DR. ROMA GANS*, Professor Emeritus of Childhood Education, Teachers College, Columbia University

DR. FRANKLYN M. BRANLEY, Chairman and Astronomer of The American Museum–Hayden Planetarium

*AVAILABLE IN SPANISH

LET'S
READ
AND
FIND
OUT

THE BLUE WHALE

On our vacation last summer, we went to Maine. My
father took me cod fishing along the coast.
Far out at sea we saw something big and black going
up and down in the water. It was the back of a
whale. Everyone was excited, even the captain of
our fishing boat. As we watched the whale, the
captain told us many things about whales.

Whales live in the sea, but they are not fish. They are warm-blooded animals like cats, cows, lions, and giraffes, and even like people.

Whales are the largest animals that have ever lived on the earth. There are many kinds of whales. The whale we saw was a fin whale. It probably weighed sixty-five tons. The blue whale is the largest whale of them all. Some blue whales weigh as much as one hundred tons. A big bus weighs only about fif-

teen tons. And some blue whales are nearly one hundred feet long. A bus is only about forty-five feet long. Whales are bigger than elephants. Some are even bigger than brontosaurus, the largest of all dinosaurs.

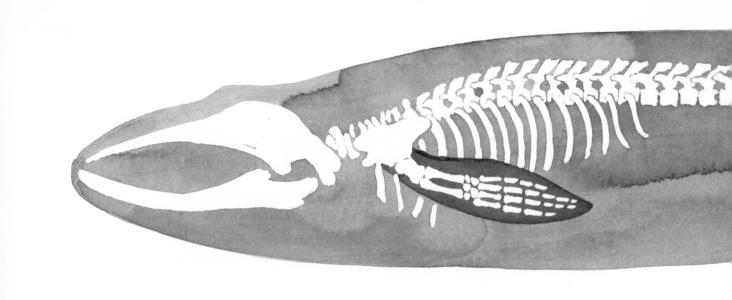

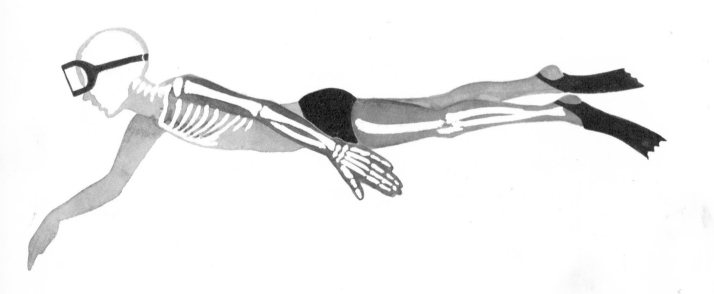

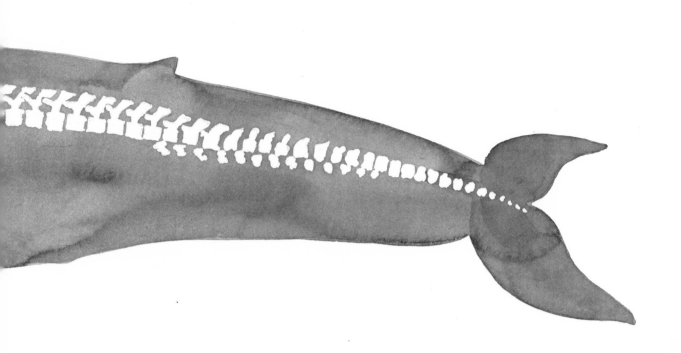

Scientists believe that the ancestors of whales lived on land millions of years ago. When whales began to live in the sea, their front legs changed into flippers. Their hind legs disappeared, and their tails grew very strong, with two big flat parts called flukes.

Whales use their flippers to steer and balance when they swim. They use their strong flukes to push themselves forward. When fish swim their tails

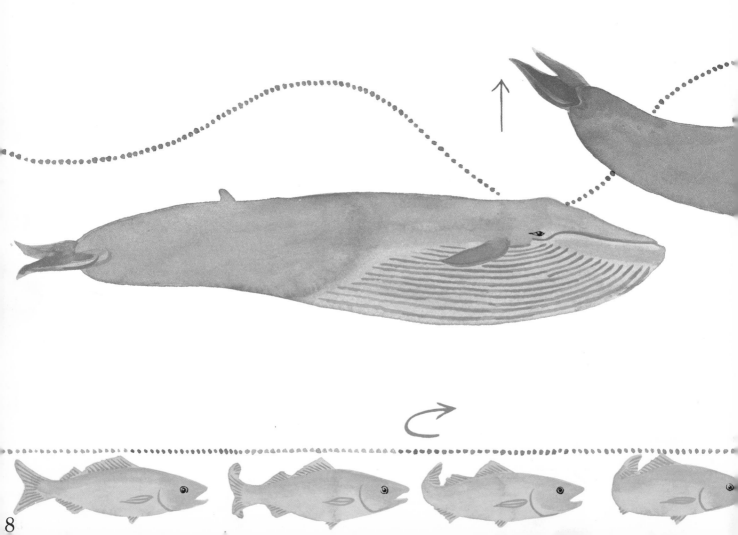

wave side to side. When whales swim their tails
flap up and down.

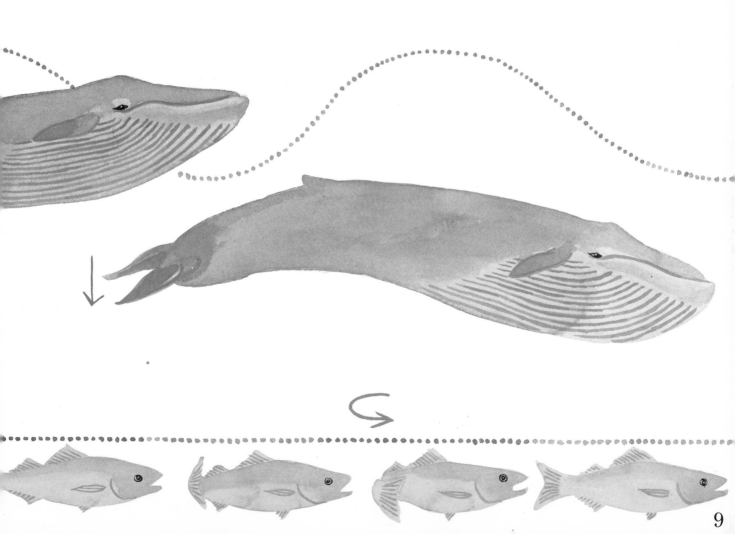

The blue whale can dive deep beneath the sea.
Some whales can stay under the water about one
   hour. But whales cannot breathe underwater the
   way fishes can. They must come up to the surface

of the sea to get air. Whales have nostrils on top of their heads. When a whale blows warm air out through its nostrils, the air is cooled suddenly. You can see the whale's breath the way you can see your breath on a cold day. From far away it looks as if the whale is spouting a fountain of seawater high into the air. When the blue whale blows its breath, the spout is twenty feet high, and sometimes higher.

Whales are mammals. They don't lay eggs. A baby blue whale grows for almost eleven months inside its mother. When a baby blue whale is born, it is about twenty-five feet long and weighs nearly two tons. That's a pretty big baby. And by the time it is one week old, the baby whale weighs twice as much as it did when it was born.

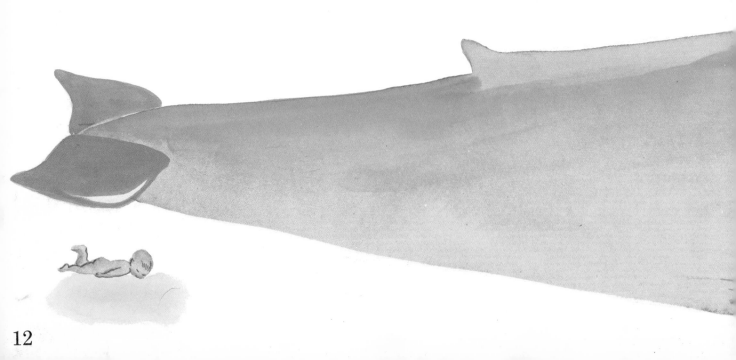

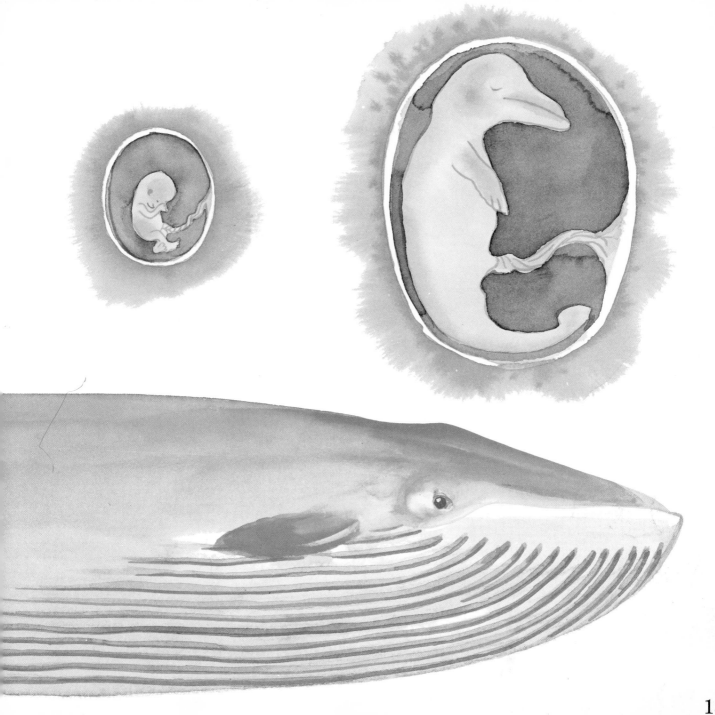

The mother whale feeds the baby more than two hundred pounds of milk every day. One hundred pounds of milk would be about two hundred big glasses.

The milk squirts through a nipple into the baby's mouth. While a mother whale nurses her baby she protects it from enemies. The mother whale almost never leaves the baby's side.

After seven months the baby blue whale leaves the mother whale. It is now about fifty-three feet long.

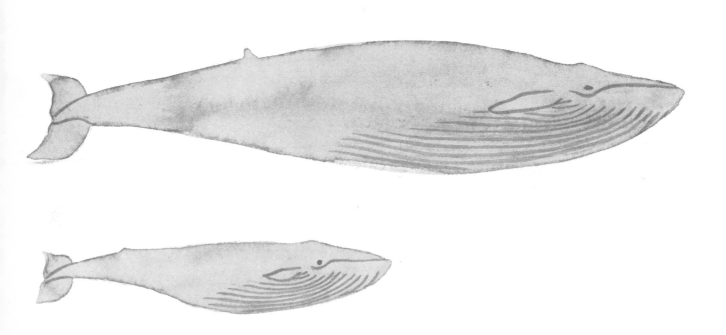

Except for men, the only natural enemies of blue whales are the killer whales. They are much smaller than blue whales. Many killer whales attack a single blue whale at the same time, so that even the largest whale cannot fight back.

In summer, blue whales live near the Arctic or Antarctic oceans. In winter, they move to slightly warmer waters.

Blue whales eat tiny shrimps called krill.

Blue whales have no teeth. Instead, plates of baleen hang from their upper jaws. These plates are close together and they have bristles on the edges. The bristles are tangled together and make a sort of sieve.

Baleen is called whalebone, but it is not a bone. It is more like a fingernail: strong as bone, easy to bend but hard to break.

When a blue whale eats, it opens its mouth and takes in a great quantity of food and water. Then it closes its mouth and raises its tongue. The water is pushed out through the baleen sieve. Millions of krill are trapped. In one big mouthful, a whale might eat five million krill.

There are many kinds of whales, and they are useful to man in different ways. Not so long ago, whalebone from some whales was used for making many things that today are made of plastic.

All whales have a thick layer of fat under their skin. The fat is called blubber. The blubber was used to make oil for lamps before we had electric lights. Today whale blubber is made into margarine, soap, face creams, and many other things.

Whale meat is used for food—some for people and
a lot for pet cats and dogs.
Because whales are so useful to man, they have been
hunted for a long time. Many whales are killed
every year.

Blue whales are already very scarce. People all around the world must protect the blue whales so they do not disappear completely.

I watched the sea. I knew there were big blue whales somewhere under the blue water. How I would like to see one!

Just then my father pulled in his fishing line. He caught a fifteen-pound codfish. That's a pretty big codfish. But it looked very small to me.

ABOUT KAZUE MIZUMURA

The author-illustrator of THE BLUE WHALE has long been interested in the world of nature and in conservation. Kazue Mizumura's previous book in the Let's-Read-and-Find-Out series, *The Emperor Penguins*, also dealt with creatures of the polar region who may be threatened by man.

Miss Mizumura is also the author and illustrator of three lovely books for young readers—*I See the Winds*, *If I Were a Mother*, and *The Way of an Ant*—and the illustrator of many more. She was born in Kamakura, Japan, and now lives in Stamford, Connecticut. She studied at the Women's Art Institute in Tokyo, as well as at Pratt Institute in Brooklyn, New York. Her busy life includes the making of ceramics and jewelry, for she believes firmly in the importance of handicrafts.